I WASN'T ALWAYS LEEANNE

An Adoption Story

a memoir by

LA Swain

Pen & Publish
Saint Louis, Missouri

Published by Pen & Publish, LLC., USA

www.PenandPublish.com
info@PenandPublish.com

Saint Louis, Missouri
(314) 827-6567

Print ISBN: 978-1-956897-14-2
e-book ISBN: 978-1-956897-15-9
Library of Congress Control Number: 2022910161

Printed on acid-free paper.

This is a book based on real memories of my childhood with no exaggerations. A collection of thoughts that tells a story as my past joins my present. Names have been changed or excluded to protect some of the people.

To my children, Stacey, Jay, and Travis—one so precious and sweet, one full of challenge and joy, and one a miracle with a gentle heart. I love you beyond words. Thank you for the smiles, hugs, kisses, and memories over the years. You were the most beautiful little people I ever laid eyes on.

"The future belongs to those who believe in the beauty of their dreams."

—Addie Philko

Contents

Introduction

Most children grow up hearing stories about the day they were born or have pictures to remember that special day. Over the years, the story of their birth is repeated, hopefully making them feel loved and special. But no one talked about the day I was born. There were no pictures of the happy couple with their new baby. No hospital photos, no celebration, no baby shower, nothing positive (or negative, for that matter) was shared with me about my birthday. There was only one picture with my mom holding me on the day she brought me home from the hospital when I was seven days old. That is my only baby photo. And for nine years, I didn't question the missing pieces.

Then when I was nine years old, I found out I was adopted and it all made sense.

Ever since that day I was told about my adoption, I felt very alone and had great anxiety about it. It was easier for me to believe that God had a purpose for me and I was put here for a reason, but it was up to me to figure it out. I needed something to hold on to at the young age of nine; I lived in a self-made fantasy world that I shared with no one, filled with unanswered questions and troubled thoughts, safe from the world's negativity. Adoption put me in a category of my own; I was different from my friends. My friends seemed to have two-parent households and memories from their past. Their minds weren't preoccupied with deep thoughts of where their parents were or why they were left to be raised by a stranger. I was ten years old, and those feelings were real. My friends were enjoying their childhood, but I was trying to process mine. I learned from them what it was like to have a real family. I felt like I couldn't talk about my feelings, even with my adopted family. When a child asks questions, it means they are ready to talk and, in my case, I was silenced. My heart ached for my birth mother in hopes that she might understand me.

I was always hopeful that I might connect with my birth family at some point in my life, most of all my birth mother, my mama. This was a wish I had longed for as long as I can remember. To me it was important to find her. It became my obsession after I got my mom's permission to follow that dream. I wasn't sure if it was even possible or if I'd succeed at all. This journey would test my patience to the point of giving up. After forty years, I was convinced it was time to move on and live out my final years without knowing anything about my birth mother or father. My most painful thought was never being able to look into my mama's face or hear her voice.

But then it happened. Things fell in place, and after all that time, the darkness was replaced with a bright light guiding me into my past. Just like that, my future awaited me.

My story goes something like this.

Chapter 1

Early Years

I was placed in a good family, a farm family. All the hospital bills had been paid in advance, but no one knows who paid those bills. The only cost was a twenty-five-dollar filing fee that my adopted parents paid for the necessary adoption paperwork. My mom and dad gave me a new name and took me home from the hospital to an older small white country house outside of Franklin, Illinois.

My mom was twenty-seven at the time she and my dad adopted me. They had been married for close to seven years when I was adopted. My mom had eloped with my dad, who was working for her father on the family farm. They had gone to high school together. One day after the elopement, my

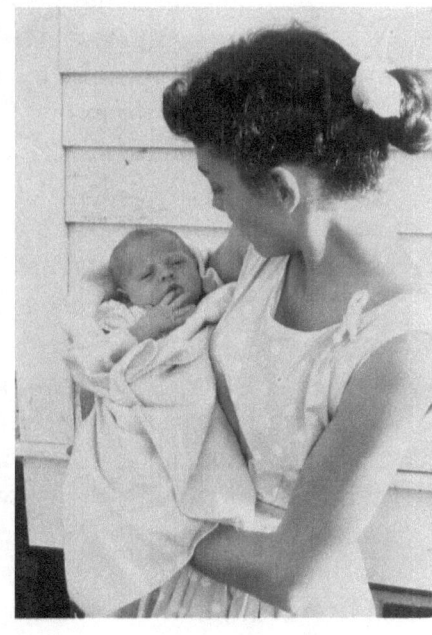

First baby photo of me at seven days old outside the Franklin house with Mom after leaving the hospital

mom's mother had found her husband quietly weeping. He had planned to walk his oldest daughter down the aisle on her wedding day, but that didn't happen and he was heartbroken.

My mom had a pretty smile and straight white teeth. She had a very slender frame with a tiny waist and was only five foot two. She had eyes of blue with dark-brown hair that she usually kept in a ponytail. She was always complaining about how hard it was to control her naturally curly hair in the Illinois humidity. I often compared her to the Coca-Cola lady in the commercials and on the tin trays. To me, she looked like a movie star. She wouldn't admit to it, but she was a very good singer with a pretty voice.

I was sixteen months old when we left our small country house in Franklin and moved to our beautiful split-level brick house in Decatur. From the back door you could see the lake. A hill led down to the waterfront, and I was told not to cross the crest of the hill. That was my boundary line—it kept me safe from the water. I always felt a little bit intimidated by the water.

My memories of life in our Decatur house mostly come from the pictures in my photo album. One photo shows my twin canopy bed that I had just transitioned into from my crib. I almost remember sleeping in that bed. There was a large corner shelf lined with toys and stuffed animals that are long gone. One was a rather large stuffed clown that was almost as big as me when I picked it up. It was made of cloth, but its face was painted on white plastic, which made it quite scary. Attached to its head was a pointed hat. I still have the squeaky, sad-faced clown that looks like Emmett Kelly. My dad must have taken it from my bedroom long ago because he had it hanging in his office when we visited him, and he gave it back to me.

In the living room, a spring pony sat in the corner. Our dining room had a mural on one wall by the table. The kitchen cabinets were knotty pine, and some of the walls matched them. During the holidays, our aluminum Christmas tree sparkled so brightly as the lights shined on it. It sat on a table out of my reach. We have pictures of a snow-covered backyard where I made a small snowman all bundled up in winter gear. I felt safe in that house and had lots of room to run about.

Fire

Our life together as a happy family came to a halt the winter after I turned two years old. Our house burned to the ground one weekend while Mom and I were away at Grandpa's house north of Jacksonville, Illinois. The house fire was accidental, they said. Our house was gone and so was my dad.

I remember the day he left us very clearly. That same day he had told us not to come home because there had been a fire. It was cold and wintery outside, just days before Christmas, when my dad arrived unexpectedly at Grandpa's house. We were only supposed to stay the weekend, but as Mom and I were packing our stuff before heading home, he walked in. The discussion took place at the end of the living room in our bedroom doorway. He was holding me in his arms as my mom wept. She was upset and had only brought enough clothes for a few days. She learned that we had lost everything at that moment; now all that was left were the things in our possession.

Mom and I would be staying at Grandpa's. I was young, but I wanted to go with my dad. He told me I had to stay with Mom, but I wasn't told where he was going or when I would see him again. Then he was gone. He just disappeared. I was left with only a few pictures of him, and one was of him standing beside his white Cadillac. To hear my mom's story, he liked that car more than he did us. When she talks, it sounds like there was some jealousy on her part—she liked that car and had to part with a lot of things she wasn't ready to part with, including him. We lost everything in that fire—it was devastating.

The one thing my dad left me that Christmas was a small keyboard piano on four metal legs. The keys were numbered so I could play from the songbook it came with. At first I had very little interest in it because I was so young. I finally grew into it and decided to practice on "Twinkle, Twinkle, Little Star." My dad had told me he would come back and hear me play after I had practiced really hard. That never happened. It was only one of his many broken promises.

The divorce happened soon after. We stayed at Grandpa's house for five years. Strangely enough, we were living with my dad's father, and he would not let my dad visit. I would assume Grandpa was ashamed of his son's poor behavior. I do know Grandpa had told my dad to stay out of my life, that I would be better off without him. If only I could have understood at the time, maybe I could have let him go sooner. Wishing for my dad to come back was a heavy thought to carry around. I feel that it had an impact on my parenting somehow. Not having my dad around took a toll on my mom, and I suppose it rebounded to affect me a great deal.

But life was good at Grandpa's house. It was a white single-family home with two bedrooms and sat on a steep hill directly off Route 78, not quite a mile outside of town. There was a barn in the back. Although it was a rural area, there were several other houses on each side of us, and the grade school I would attend when I reached school age was just across the highway.

Most of my childhood memories are of living here with Grandpa. He basically raised me and loved me. He had a kind heart letting us stay and keeping a roof over our heads. Grandpa gave me a nickname, Tootsie, and it stuck with me all through my school years and into adulthood. Toots, a very small, shy, quiet girl with long blonde hair and blue eyes.

It was very obvious Grandpa loved me dearly from his kindness and concern over my well-being. He had arthritis so bad, and his feet were swollen, making it hard for him to navigate. He was a retired mailman and had served in World War I. We had a close bond, and he enjoyed my company and spent time watching me from his lawn chair outside. I had a black pony named Blackie and lots of cats. I loved my swing set outside the back door and spent a lot of time out there. I would swing high while singing nursery rhymes at the top of my lungs. One day I swallowed a bug. I don't remember getting sick from it, but my grandma, Mom's mother, said it could make me sick.

Across the pasture was my dad's sister, who had almost adopted me. She had signed up on a church list to adopt a baby, but when she got the call there was a baby available for adoption, she was pregnant with her first child. You might say she surrendered me to her brother, my dad, who had been added to the waiting list. In only a few short years she had several young children of her own, all younger than me, and they would come over to play during our time at Grandpa's house.

My dad had left with the Cadillac, so those days Mom drove a gray Ford car from the forties. I'm not sure where this car came from or who it may have belonged to, but it reminded me of a giant Volkswagen Bug. It had wool seats that were scratchy, and each time you would open the doors you could smell the wool. It's hard to describe—somewhat of a dusty smell. A few times Mom let me sit on her lap and put the car in the garage. She would straighten the wheels so all I had to do was put my hands on the steering wheel. It made me feel important.

Mom and I shared a bedroom at Grandpa's house. We each had twin beds, but in the middle of the night, I would crawl into her bed. On one particular night when I was not quite four years old, I was snuggling down waiting to drift off to sleep in Mom's bed when a sense of curiosity came over me. I sat up and peeked over her shoulder. What I saw was the most beautiful, bright white figure, and it was watching us sleep. I tried to blink it away, but it stayed very quiet, not moving at all. I laid down, unsure of what was happening. I couldn't believe what I was seeing, and for a brief moment I thought my mom was dying. When I sat up to have another look, it had disappeared. It never came back. I lay there thinking till I fell asleep.

The next morning, I asked Mom if she had seen that lady by our bed last night. I told her she was watching us sleep. She ignored me, said no, and went on about her business. Did I see an angel? I know I did. My very own guardian angel came to check on me that night. It was a one-time sighting, and I felt blessed.

In 2019, I drew the image of my guardian angel I saw that night and had it printed on canvas.

Missing Daddy

After my dad left, I pleaded with my mom to see him for months. His whereabouts were unknown, and it took a while for Mom to locate him. But soon we were on the way to visit him at his workplace just months after that terrible day. He was an insurance man at an office in Decatur. The meeting was short, but I was satisfied for the moment.

I don't have many memories with my dad. Most of the memories I do have come from a few pictures I had in a photo book rather than actual time I spent with him. From those pictures, I knew he was tall and handsome with dark hair; he wore a smile and was charming. His build was on the stocky side, and he didn't stay in one place for very long, making it hard for us to find him. Perhaps that was his plan all along to keep his distance far from our location. My most vivid memories when I was around him were the smell of beer on his breath and the day he left us at Grandpa's house. A memory of his betrayal to us.

My dad had a brother, my uncle, and he tried to fill the void my dad had made. He dropped off small gifts for me or sent a card from time to time to make me feel that someone cared. My uncle was a dentist in a small town close by. During one of his visits to Grandpa's house I had my first loose tooth. I walked up to him with a big smile on my face and showed him my loose tooth, and he took his thumb and popped that tooth plumb out of my mouth. I was in tears. It didn't hurt, but I had wanted to pull my first loose tooth by myself. I was discouraged.

The next time I saw Dad was the summer before my seventh birthday. He visited Grandpa's house and brought his family of three children. That was the day everything finally fell in place—I figured it out. I was just too young to understand, but deeply I missed what most children would, a solid family with a mom and dad. He made a promise to be my dad. He had signed the paperwork to adopt me, a commitment, but for him it wasn't enough. He had failed to keep his end of the deal and would let his new family down just as he had us in the years to come. Soon his new family would be unable to locate him too.

After this meeting, my dad disappeared for eighteen years. I found it hard to accept all the special moments he was not around to share and, of course, I missed the idea of having a dad. My mom didn't talk about her relationship with my dad. I could tell it was painful for her. I later found out he and Mom were married for quite a few years and had lost several pregnancies and then lost the ability to even conceive a child. That's when I entered their lives.

Life at Grandma's

It seemed I was sick most of the time while living with Grandpa. Those were my childhood days, and I caught anything and everything imaginable. Tonsillitis, bronchitis, chickenpox, even three types of measles. It seemed to me that I would always be sick.

When I was seven, we left Grandpa's house and moved in with my mom's parents, and I had to have my tonsils taken out. What an unpleasant experience that was. It took four nurses to hold me down for the pre-op shot, and afterward I couldn't stop throwing up. I was freaking out because it was pure blood. In those days when your tonsils were removed, they used stitches, and the nurses worried I would rupture my sutures. I suppose I had a reaction to the medicines they had used. Finally they gave me some medicine to reverse the effects I was having.

Grandma was patient with me, and I felt her love every day we lived with her. She let me play in the flour on the kitchen counter with small toys, making roads and pretend cooking. I followed her all about the house, watching her cook meals, clean the house, or work in the garden. I was full of questions, and she so kindly explained everything she did. Sometimes you could hear a chuckle in her voice. She was the only grandma I had, and she was the best.

Even with such supportive grandparents, I know how hard it must have been for my mom to raise me alone without financial help from my dad. It must have been a heavy burden, and it showed in her actions. She was unhappy and tearful, lacking confidence. Earning money wasn't easy for her; she hated every job she had. I felt like I was part of the problem as she reminded me how much it cost her when I was sick all the time. It was hard not to take it personally. If she was in a mood, she wasn't very nice and talking to me was not soothing to her. I internalized a lot and I learned not to be bitter like her. It made me think how I might handle the situation if I were the adult. Perhaps she would always hold on to those grudges.

On a few occasions, I shared my concern with Grandma about my mom's unhappiness and how it made me feel. Her response was, "Your mom's had a difficult life, and she was dealt a bad deck of cards." I could understand that, but my mom made those choices and it seemed wrong to take it out on me.

Nevertheless, Grandma and I had a good time hanging out together. When she sat down in her chair, she usually fell asleep while reading the newspaper. When the sun went down, she would look out her window by her chair and, binoculars in hand, watch the movie from the drive-in movie theater just down the road. On July 4, fireworks were set off in the parking lot of the drive-in. Even though it was loud, it was fun to watch the fireworks from Grandma's front yard. Our whole family got together to celebrate, and cars lined the road on both sides.

I always thought we moved to Grandma's house because my mom had started dating and it wasn't proper to stay at the in-laws' anymore. But as a kid, I missed Grandpa so much and wanted to visit him. When I asked to see him, I was told he had died. I sobbed uncontrollably. I hadn't told him goodbye. They told me he was in the hospital and that little people weren't allowed to visit. It was my aunt, the one who almost adopted me, who saved the day. She told me when she visited Grandpa in the hospital, the last thing he said to her was, "How's my little Tootsie?" That's all it took to ease my troubled mind. It healed me instantly, and even if it wasn't true, it was thoughtful.

Chapter 2

New Family in the Making

Mom had met a man who was quiet and kind. He listened to me, laughed with me, and spent time with me. He was just nice. He had milk cows, and I learned how to milk them. I watched him work with the sheep and had my first encounter with a hot barbed wire fence. OUCH!

She married that man on August 14, 1964. I had just turned nine years old the week before, and boy was this a big change. My mom and stepfather left me alone for a week with Grandma to go on their honeymoon. I was devastated. I had never been alone somewhere without my mom. It had always been the two of us for as long as I could remember. Shortly after my mom and new step-father returned from their trip, we moved again. I would move a total of six times the first ten years of my life and change schools four times.

We began our new family with my stepfather's two daughters north of Jacksonville, Illinois, in the small town of Literberry just off Route 78. The house we lived in was owned by my stepfather's father. It was very old and not modernized. Truth is, it was too small for all of us, but they said it was a starter place and we would make it work. His two older girls used the dining room as their bedroom, and I'm pretty sure my bedroom was a large closet. We hung material in the open doorways to create some sense of privacy. I might add it had no running water and no bathroom. We had an outhouse not far from the backdoor and a red pump sitting on the kitchen sink top. This was our only water source in the house. We had to heat water on the stove and take a bird bath from a pan of water.

One hot August night while we lay sleeping with all the windows open in our new quiet little town just shortly after we were settled in, we were startled awake by people shouting and fireworks going off all around our house. We sprang from our beds in fear and huddled in the tiny living room. I was crying from all the commotion, and my stepfather picked me up in his arms and began running around the house shouting for the people outside to stop. When that failed, he put me down and ran out the front door to confront them and demanded that they stop immediately. As he returned inside the house, I noticed he was wearing nothing but his white undershorts. I thought nothing of it because that night he became my hero—he was brave! I knew this was the best dad that any little girl could want. When all had quieted down, we were able to go back to bed.

The next morning, my stepfather went outside to check for damage. What he found was a display of ladies' underwear hanging from a clothesline on our rooftop. We had just experienced a shivaree. My stepfather's friends and cousins had joined in to welcome us into our new place by playing a prank on the newlyweds—in the middle of the night! Apparently, that made it even better and funnier. Trust me, it was not. As funny as it sounds, we never spoke of that night again. Now that I'm older, it's a fond memory. I knew after that night my stepfather would be there forever and do anything for us. He was going to be around for a long time. And . . . he was!

My stepfather was a very good role model. I was never able to call him "dad" to his face because it seemed strange—he was my stepfather. He was happy to be my dad and left it up to me what I wanted to call him. I used every opportunity to call him my dad when I talked about him. I was proud of him; he was a hardworking guy.

My mom and stepfather offered to change my last name so we would all match, but I declined. Changing my name would change who I was, and it wasn't me who had married, it was my mom. That's how I processed it at the time. Changing my name would make finding me impossible; I had grown into my name and that is who I had become to classmates or anyone, for that matter.

I was delighted to have two new sisters even though they were older than me. They were as different as night and day. One short and the other one tall. They didn't look alike at all, not even a little. They seemed close to each other. I tried to connect with them, but it wasn't easy, and I felt like I was a huge bother. There was a bit of tension in the air; I guess I needed them more than they needed me. They had lost their mother to leukemia and weren't ready for any more changes. I remember thinking how terrible that was for them. They didn't require much attention and seemed eager to leave home.

My stepsisters became independent and moved out of the house, and after that they rarely returned. During the holidays they would join us, but only for short periods of time. Meanwhile, I had a lot of growing up to do, and I resumed my life as an only child. Some of the new family members and a few classmates called me spoiled. I had not heard that word before. It seemed like a very old-fashioned thing to say. They must have assumed that as an only child I automatically had everything my heart desired. Quite the opposite—we lost everything in the fire. Talk like that made me feel insignificant; they didn't know me or my situation. I didn't ask for much at all. I was content. I wasn't demanding and had refused an allowance when it was offered to me. I would adapt and try to blend in.

Shattered

In less than a year we left that house for a bigger one a few miles south of Virginia, Illinois, along Route 78, just in time to start a new school. This house was huge, a white two-story farmhouse. We had three bedrooms with many windows and a few smaller rooms upstairs that had been used for farm workers in the early days. There was even an extra stairway that led down to the back porch, a private entrance. We lived here until a few weeks before I graduated. We settled into a new routine; it was consistent. Each day we cared for cows, pigs, ducks, cats, dogs, and a pony. In the back pasture was a small pond for the cows to drink. I spent a lot of time walking those pastures, fishing in that pond, and playing along the banks of the small Indian Creek that ran through the property.

One lazy day I was full of questions about our newly formed family. My mom and I were sitting on my bedroom floor talking. I felt excited and curious. I was asking about the girls, wondering where they came from and where I came from. And then she told me. I couldn't believe what I was hearing. My life was a lie; I was adopted. I would never know my real mother or father. My mom tried to reassure me that my birth mother loved me and it must have broken her heart to give me away. My birth mother probably wanted me to have something better, something she was unable to give me. When I asked Mom how much I weighed at birth, it was a question she had no answer for; she told me she didn't know. When I asked what time of day I was born, again she had no answer; it wasn't her memory to tell. It broke my heart and my spirit. My birth certificate was an adapted version after the adoption, and this information was not included. Fifteen years would pass before these questions were answered.

Our close bond was shattered that day. There was a distance between me and my mom that I can't explain. There were too many changes in such a short time. I had recently learned the tooth fairy didn't exist, the Easter Bunny wasn't real, and guess what, Santa Claus wasn't real either! Now, neither was my mom.

I hoped the next morning I would wake up to find the whole conversation had been a nightmare. Maybe, just maybe, my mom would tell me it was all a joke and none of it was true. She was good at jokes. "Lighten up," she would say. "It's only a joke, can't you take a joke?" Most times I thought it was cruel and hurtful, but this time I welcomed a different outcome. But it didn't happen.

My relationship with my mom seemed toxic from that day on. We just didn't connect; her personality was that of indifference. The lack of emotion and a nurturing soul made situations uncomfortable. Of course, she was kind and did nice things, but there was no closeness after that day. All these questions I had bottled up inside me still needed answers. She started to get short. I suppose she had become uncomfortable after our lengthy talk.

I felt isolated; a child shouldn't feel so empty. Where did I belong? Those words, engraved in me forever. Perhaps my mom was even sorry she had told me. I now believe that raising me was too much for her to handle as a single parent. I started to feel more like a possession than a person. Things started to make sense over time. She would judge me by the look on my face and would tell me, "Wipe that look off your face." This was the face I was born with, and those comments hurt—I couldn't change my face. We didn't have productive conversations and instead had disagreements about my views being different from hers. She had little regard for my choices or concerns on most matters.

Over time, I found my mom to be emotionally immature from some of her statements and actions. We shouldn't rely on others to find happiness. I felt punished by my mom's unhappiness brought on by her own choices. We don't choose our parents. They choose us. She didn't choose me; I was handed to her because someone else changed their mind.

I kept thinking nobody wanted me. Why did so many people walk out on me? I felt displaced, being denied the opportunity of a birth family with siblings. My past did not exist. I had no story, no pictures from the day I was born, and most of my baby pictures were burned in the Decatur house fire. The news of my adoption left me anxious with a lot of thoughts to process.

Princess the Pony

I got a pony soon after Mom told me I was adopted. I often wonder if that's why I got a pony, to keep me occupied. I hadn't asked for one like most children might. Perhaps it was a way to get my mind off of things to keep me busy. Her previous owners had named her Princess. She was the best pony and my best friend.

The first summer I had her, she won a blue ribbon at the local 4-H fair. That proud little pony was all stretched out with her tail arched high. She took everyone's attention and was very worthy of that ribbon. Someone asked if I put ginger under her tail for her to perform so perfectly. I had no idea what they were talking about and told them that's just how she is. She was a show pony. (Apparently, when you apply ginger under the tail of a pony, it makes them hold their tail high due to its irritating properties. I was unaware of this at the time.)

I spent lots of time with Princess and adored her. If I wasn't riding her, I was brushing her or lying next to her while she was resting on the grass. She was so warm, and she would nibble on me as if she were giving me a kiss. She was tied to a concrete block, giving her plenty of room to move about, and we kept a close eye on her. She would munch on grass all day long. She was able to move herself about the yard to reach new grass. I gave her sugar water; she was fond of sugar cubes too. She never ran off; she knew we were close by and would nicker when she saw us. She was just happy mowing the grass with her teeth all day long. At night, we put her in a fenced lot by the barn beside the pigs so she had company and was safe.

She was an average size, not small but not big. She had a white body with brown patches all over her and a pretty marked face. You might say she had a sweet face and good disposition. If you scratched her tummy, she would stretch out her neck and wiggle her top lip. I could do anything with this pony.

I started out riding her with a saddle that seemed too small for her, but it worked. Most of the time I rode her bareback. We would take off down the edge of the road at a mere walk. I would try to encourage her to move faster, even a trot would do, but she was in total control. When we turned around to head home, we were at a fast run, and it was a hang-on-for-life kind of run. As long as I was prepared, we made it back in one piece, but if I'd fallen off I do believe she would have kept going without me. She meant the world to me; we were faithful companions. A few times in the spring when she was feeling spunky, she would put her head down and give a little hop, then I was on the ground. Luckily, I didn't have far to fall.

Princess, wearing sunglasses and posing for her picture

Growing Up

After my mom told me I was adopted, we fell into a rut. The days when we could have gone to town or anywhere to have fun, we stayed home no matter the weather. Mom watched her TV soap operas and sitcoms. She enjoyed her many books and magazines. Her books were her best friends, but I wanted so badly to be her best friend. We made weekly trips to the grocery store, and that became our routine. I looked forward to each day we went shopping because it was a treat to leave the house.

Over time, it seemed that Mom showed no sense of pride for my accomplishments. When she was angry, I would hear, "You don't appreciate anything people do for you." She used sarcasm quite often with me but was super sweet to others in the same room. I was shocked by the outbursts because I had appreciated everything. Obviously, she internalized her unhappiness under layers of depression, isolating herself and saying she needed her solitude of peace and quiet. The thing that hurt the most was hearing "I should have left you on that doorstep." After a while, I became numb, and the words didn't mean so much. It's just Mom having a bad day. I'd walk away, find something to do, and stay out of her way. We did have some good times, but those memories happened long before I started school. I suppose the newness of me wore off like that of a new puppy. A puppy soon grows up, and so did I.

From the day I learned I was adopted, I began thinking about my birth mother. That one question remained, why? Why would someone give away a baby? It was my first time hearing the word *adopted*. In an effort to be helpful, my mom told me of another little girl who was adopted; I remember how it seemed that her parents were so nice to her and her family seemed so happy. They were very involved with the children. For whatever reason, my mom and I couldn't work things out and be friends; I did try, but she seemed so angry. I thought for sure there was a good reason my birth mother chose to give me away, and I wanted to know. I stayed positive and internalized many feelings. It was a constant thought I couldn't shake off. Surely, my real family would understand me. Did I look like them? Did they miss me? Did they love me? I tried to suppress the thoughts and move on. People would make comments from time to time, "Boy, you look like your mother." I couldn't think of anything to say. It would only remind me that it wasn't possible, so I said nothing.

All I wanted to do was make my birth mother proud of me. I needed a plan, a positive goal. I would be strong for her. One might say that in her absence I gained my strength. Regardless of the troubled times, I would always think of her. If she could live without me, I could find a way to live without her.

I learned of my adoption just months before entering a new grade school. My new classmates would ask me, "Where are you from?" I would say "I don't know, I'm adopted." It hadn't occurred to me to say Jacksonville and keep it simple. These same class-mates told me I talked with an accent, so of course I was curious to where it came from. In my days of growing up during the sixties, making a new friend was a big deal. Parents wanted to know who their children were hanging out with. They needed to know who the parents were, where they were from, what job they had, and if they were good people. It was critical. On a few occasions, I ran into some small-minded people who would say, we don't know her parents, so it's best to stay away. This led me to believe more than ever that I needed to find my birth mother so I would have those answers.

I spent years trying to fit into other people's families, desperate to find my own. I was filled with insecurity and anxiety, wondering how different life might have been if I had been raised by my birth family. Hoping they were good people and not criminals. My mind was mixed with terrible scenarios of what might have happened.

Without a background, I was merely a transplant. Even a trip to the doctor's office was traumatic. What? No family history? I remember how worried I was when I heard in high school we would be making a family tree. All the kids seemed so happy to embrace the challenge. I was devastated. The family I was placed with didn't talk about past generations or descendants. I lived in a very closed world and wasn't exposed to a larger family unit. We had holidays with family but only immediate members. We didn't travel or get out much, at least not far from home. I wasn't part of any group activities—living in the country was inconvenient. I was so relieved when I found out we weren't required to make a family tree for class. I was glad because my family tree wasn't my own, and at that moment, I wanted one so badly.

Chapter 3

Paperwork

Once I was out of school and working my first job, I would find myself out looking around crowds, hoping to see someone I might resemble. I figured my mama would look like me. In my mind, she was only a few small towns away from where I lived in Central Illinois. I had been told I had a twin in a neighboring town on numerous occasions. Occasionally when a person would tell me, "You look just like your mother," I would respond with, "That's funny, I'm adopted," and we would laugh about it. Not that it was funny; it relieved a tense moment, and I could make my getaway.

When I had my first baby, it became even more important for me to try to locate my birth mother. After having my own child, I couldn't imagine how you would give one away. Mom gave me her permission to begin the search for my birth mother, as I was sure she would.

In 1979, I welcomed my second child, my first son. After his birth, I took a break from the search for my birth mother to adapt to raising two small children. When I started my search again, I contacted some of the places and people that my mom said were involved in my adoption for information but came up empty-handed. A lot of time had passed, making it more difficult. Most of the people involved in my birth and adoption had died.

Everywhere I went, paperwork was securely locked away. People looked at me like I had two heads when I started to question how to obtain my birth and adoption records. In those days, no one seemed to agree with snooping around. *Leave things alone,* they'd say. *You might find something you don't want to know.* I contacted legal aid and still found nothing. This search for my birth mother was not going to be quick or easy and, in all honesty, it was extremely difficult. I suppose that was the whole idea of giving away a child. I became frustrated.

I collected ideas from several people and realized I should attempt to obtain my original birth certificate, but even that would need a court order. The next step would be to open my adoption papers. The attorney that sealed my adoption papers was still in practice, so Mom and I headed to his office. He was helpful and said the papers were not in his possession; the files had been moved to the courthouse, and he suggested I talk to the judge there so my records could be released to me legally. Collecting papers and getting permission took time, so much time. It wasn't until after my third child was born that I finally held my sealed adoption papers in my hands.

The Birth of My Third Child

In 1980, my third child was born seventeen months after my second child. This time something was wrong: his heart wasn't working. He had transposition of the great vessels, a serious condition requiring surgery. The hospital wasn't able to treat him, and he had to be transferred to a bigger hospital.

He was flown by helicopter to the Chicago Children's Hospital, just off North Lakeshore Drive on Fullerton Avenue. It was a scary twenty-four hours. The team of doctors at the children's hospital had treated other babies with this condition and was prepared to keep him stable until his surgery. These doctors were filled with such empathy; they were professional and treated us like family.

It was a very serious situation, and there was nothing I could do but wait by the phone. We had to find a way to get to Chicago. My baby was so far away from us. It was a lot to process, and life would never be the same afterward.

Although it was touch and go, the surgery was a success! That little guy was home one month after his birthday, just in time for Christmas. He met his brother and sister for the first time. My oldest boy spoke his first full sentence once the baby got home. He woke one morning and walked by his new baby brother sitting in his pumpkin seat, and I heard this little voice say, "Hi dare, baby." I smiled and asked, "What did you say?" and he repeated the phrase. How sweet! They've been close ever since.

Our schedule was full of medicines and doctor visits for follow-up care, not just on the new baby but for everyone. It took him a year to recover, and we went back and forth to Chicago each year for follow-up visits.

During this time, I kept wishing I knew more about my family's medical history. (Although in my son's case, it wouldn't have made any difference.) The experience made me even more determined to find my birth family.

My Original Birth Certificate

After things settled down and we fell back into a routine at home, I resumed my search for my birth mother. My first step was getting my original birth certificate after the courts had ordered for it to be released.

I stood at the state archives building in Springfield, Illinois, waiting for my original birth certificate to be released. It seemed like hours passed before the man returned to the counter and handed me a piece of paper. As I read the paper, my heart sank. All the information I needed was crossed out and replaced with "legally omitted."

My original birth certificate did say the exact time I was born and how much I weighed. That was incredible news—I had waited years to learn something most people take for granted.

The birth certificate also said which states my parents were from and my parents' ages. Their ages confused me, but regardless I needed to know. I had hoped to learn more from the birth certificate, like their names or addresses, but at least I now knew that my mama was not a local person—she was from New York, five states away. That made my search for her an even harder task than I originally thought.

My Adoption Papers

The next step in my plan was to open my adoption papers using the court order provided by the judge, and then proceed to the doctor's office and hospital for more paperwork. All these papers combined would surely be useful in the search.

I opened my adoption papers with great anticipation. Finally, my mama's name. I began to feel real; I discovered I had been given the name D. J. at birth. The questions in my mind started all over again. Why did my adopted parents change my name? I like the one I was given at birth; it matched my mama's name. My mom told me her story: she and my dad wanted me to be theirs, so they gave me a name that they agreed upon. Lee from my dad and Anne from Mom, and the new Miss America for 1955 was Lee Ann Meriwether. That's how the name originated. I had to admit it did seem like a good idea.

With my mama's name in hand, I dug into phone books and yearbooks at schools and colleges in our local area, trying to find anyone who might know her. I learned the last name was not common in this area and that people were rude. People don't like it when you knock on their door and ask if they know a lady by the name of ——. I utilized the telephone operators in the states where each parent had been born and found a whole bunch of people out east who shared this last name. The number of people who shared the last name made it harder to track down my family or make any calls.

I searched for my birth announcement in old newspapers at the local library on the microfiche files to see who else was born while I was in the hospital as an infant. Mothers used to stay in the hospital as long as a week after giving birth, if not longer, back in the day. I was unable to find my own birth announcement or any others that were of use. It was sad not finding a birth announcement for me but understandable. Brick walls are hard to break down, and hearts are easily shattered. But looking through those newspaper files, I did come across an article about the terrible storm that happened the night I greeted the world.

Records from the Doctor's Office

With my court order in hand and high hopes it would still be valid, I headed to the office of the doctor who delivered me. My original birth certificate had been signed by him, and I had a court order stating I could view my birth mother's records at his office.

A colleague of the doctor led me to a dark room in the back of the office and said, "This is against my better judgment, and I'm being forced to do this by the courts. I don't approve. You can look but take no copies of anything at all."

Nothing was to leave the room. All I could do was look over those precious papers. I had nothing to write on, no pen, paper, nothing! He was rude. It made me feel unworthy. I was about to peek into my past, where it all began. I found information about my birth mother's immediate family. She had a mother, father, three brothers, and a sister. Her mother, my grandmother, was a twin. I didn't stay long; the staff at the doctor's office made this visit very uncomfortable, and soon I left the building. Once again, all I found was another brick wall. I was discouraged to say the least and feeling troubled.

I now knew the states my parents were born in, my mama's name, and the members in her immediate family. I searched and searched for information at the library. I looked at yearbooks from the local high school and college to see if my mama, her sister, or anyone with her last name had gone to school in the area but found nothing.

One day while visiting Mom's house, we were listening to the local radio station. They were talking about having a psychic, Greta Alexander, on their program once a week for an hour. She had helped police solve a few cases when they had run out of leads. The radio show would accept phone calls from anyone with questions, and she would do a reading over the phone. I made a few calls but was on hold forever. My calls were never answered; they were busy with other callers. I'm sure Mom knew we would not succeed, but she played along very well. Before you knew it, they announced, "That's all we have time for today, folks."

I hold a deep appreciation for the lady that raised me and everything she did or went through for the two of us. I carry a commitment beyond what most family members do. Over the years, Mom assured me that she knew nothing about my birth mother or her situation. When I asked her if I could look for my birth mother, she didn't appear upset. How does a person respond to such a question? I felt this to be a genuine heart-to-heart conversation; Mom was calm and forthcoming. It seemed it would be our last in-depth talk.

The thought of finding my mama consumed me. It would be hard to find someone that may not want to be found. It would also take forever and be overwhelming. The years flew by as life got busier. Still I was haunted by these thoughts: Where's my birth mother? Who do I look like? Who do I act like? Where do I go from here?

Letting Go of Daddy

Meanwhile, it had been decades since I had seen my dad. My aunt, who almost adopted me, arranged a visit with him because she knew it had been important to me years before. For whatever reason, when the opportunity came up to see him, I thought it was a good idea to visit and catch up. I was in for a huge awakening.

That day, I learned I had wasted my time wishing for the impossible to happen after all those years. My dad only cared about himself, not us or me. He explained to me how he needed to move on and have kids of his own, and he told me that I should understand now that I had my own children. He said he always thought the grass was greener on the other side of the fence. To me, this was nothing but a bad excuse for his behavior. All those years that I missed him and wished he had been a part of my life had been a waste of my energy. He had a charm about him, so of course I missed him when I was younger, but everything changed that day when he showed me he didn't care. What he did was unforgivable, and I could finally forget. I meant nothing to him. Maybe I knew this all along and was in denial, but it was hard that day as I crossed the bridge of acceptance. Now I could move forward and leave my childhood behind me. There was no changing the past, just changing the way I reacted to it.

I was heartbroken by his poor character and never wanted to make contact again. We had driven two hours to see him, and it was a long drive home. He made several attempts to reconnect in the coming years, but I didn't allow it to happen. We spoke a few times on the phone, but he hadn't changed. He wanted nothing to do with me other than to share his bachelorhood stories, and I couldn't wait for him to hang up. I didn't want my children exposed to his behavior or have to explain his actions ever again. That was a bad experience. I was so grateful to have my own children, and I loved each one of them so much—they are my world. It could be difficult at times, but they were the best thing that ever happened in my life. I often wished I had a better example of what normal parenting was like to apply to my own children. I know I made mistakes and I wasn't sure if it was my lack of knowledge or my own shortcomings.

Many years would pass before I was inspired to search for my birth mother again.

My Mama's Hospital Records

My son's heart condition gave me a window of opportunity to seek more paperwork about my adoption and family history, like my mama's hospital records. It was my last resort. In November 1993, I was granted a court order to open my mama's hospital records at the time of delivery. I hurried home to see what I had uncovered. I was so excited to see my baby footprint and my mama's thumbprint side by side. It would have been so nice to have on that day I was told I was adopted.

My birth mother's hospital records also listed a local address that she was staying at when she gave birth to me. At this point, I had a lot of knowledge. I knew Mama's name, age, family members, and home state, and now I had the address she had stayed at the time I was born. But I didn't know where to go from there. I had no current location. New York is a big state. Women get married and change their last name. I would need to give this great thought before moving on.

I used the library to find out who lived in or owned the house that my mama had lived at when she had me. When I arrived at the address, however, the house was unoccupied. Another dead end. I returned to the library to find out who the current owners were and where they lived. My search led me to a woman named Sarah who lived nearby the house that was listed on my mama's hospital records. I headed to her house in hopes of talking to her.

Talking to Sarah

I stood on the doorstep to Sarah's house, nervous and excited at the same time. She answered the door, and I explained who I was. She gasped, then welcomed me into her home. Sarah was excited to say the least, and it made me feel special knowing she had met my mama. She was a very kind and sweet lady. As she hugged me close, she motioned me to sit.

Sarah said she had always thought about me and wondered what had become of me. She recollected her memories of that time, and I shared the information I'd gathered from different places. Everything seemed to match up.

At the time of my birth, Sarah and her husband were living in the rental house and would rent out rooms occasionally to someone in need. Her husband was a truck driver, gone for long periods of time. My mama and her sister had arrived in Jacksonville on June 10, 1956, and had traveled all the way from New York with only four hundred dollars to live on until they could return home.

The girls were barely out of school and didn't appear out of place in the college town. They had no family or friends in Jacksonville. My mama and her sister had gone to a lot of trouble to get here, and they were determined to keep the situation hidden from everyone.

The girls kept to themselves; they took walks and went to a grocery store down the street. They had a car but said the sister was afraid to drive at night. Sarah thought she remembered a man coming by to check on the girls once a week and pay the rent for the room they were staying in. Sarah confirmed that my mama's mother, my grandmother, was a twin. She was married to their father, my grandfather, and my mama and sister had three brothers.

The girls had remained fairly quiet until the night of my birth, the night with the bad storm. The night I was born, Sarah spoke with Mama's sister, who was so excited following my delivery. Her most precious memory to me was that my mama had held me after I was born. Sarah was sure my mama didn't want to leave me. To Sarah, it sounded like my mama's only option, the best one for all parties. The girls would soon head east, leaving the baby for someone else to raise. It was the best thing to do.

Sarah's enthusiasm was more than enough to satisfy me from our brief meeting. Even so, I was left on the open plains of Central Illinois and now had more information than ever about my past. But I still wanted to meet my mama.

Chapter 4

Putting the Pieces Together

Through all my research and paperwork trails, I was finally able to put together my birth story. It meant so much to me to finally know about the day of my birth and know my own past.

My story began like most good stories do, on a dark and stormy night. Storms in Central Illinois happen quite often during the summers. The heat and humidity build up until the sky quickly darkens and breaks loose with a downpour of rain, thunder, and lightning that soon make you cover your eyes and ears. The wind spins you sideways with the smell of corn pollinating in the nearby fields. This is the kind of storm that knocks out the power to most of the town and surrounding areas, the kind of storm that reminds you of the power of nature, how small you are in the world.

It was storming so strongly that the hospital generator kicked on as I greeted the world in August 1956 in Jacksonville. The hospital record shows I was admitted at 8:21 p.m., but the birth certificate reads Baby Girl Horton, born at 8:19 p.m. They recorded my footprint and my mama's thumbprint. My mama held me after I was born, then headed back to New York with her sister a week later.

My adoption was a private arrangement between the doctor, hospital, and the local Methodist church. It was the sheriff's job to hand off the baby (me) to my adoptive parents just seven days after

I was born. I began my new life with my mom and dad. My mama was not aware that she could have come back for me within a year.

Sharing My Story with My Children

I tried to be a good mom; I was a divorced, single parent making the best of it. I had a full-time job, and raising three children while keeping a roof over our heads was hard. I sometimes think I failed to connect with my own children. At times it was difficult; work was demanding, and so were they. These three children were good kids; they were my everything. I tried to be the best example for them. I gave all the love I had to them, but still it takes so much more to raise a family.

When my three children were in junior high and high school, I realized that I wanted to share my story with them. Their whole life revolved around the family we had made. Deep bonds were set in place and tucked away with love and security, and I felt they could handle the situation I was about to share with them as adults.

We had a group huddle in our kitchen, the four of us, and I gathered my thoughts and shared my story of being adopted as a baby. My children became intrigued and asked many questions, and I answered in the best way I knew how, with honesty. They seemed to be good with it. We were too busy to dwell on it. I felt a sense of relief knowing that I had someone to talk to if I stumbled upon the truth of my birth family somewhere along the way.

My three children all grown up in April 2019

Still Trying

I was desperate to find my mama any way I could. I wrote a letter to the TV show *Unsolved Mysteries* explaining my situation. They replied that they couldn't help me. Once again, I hit a dead end. *Unsolved Mysteries* included a list of agencies designed to help adopted people find their birth parents. I couldn't use any of the suggestions because my adoption was not through any agencies that had a paperwork trail.

Years later, a law was passed that allowed adopted people to register with the Illinois Adoption Registry and Medical Information Exchange. If or when any family member tried to contact a surrendered baby, they could leave information with the registry and not have direct contact. It required only a little paperwork to sign up, so I did. I couldn't imagine it would amount to anything since my name had been changed at birth, but I hoped it might get me one step closer to meeting my mama.

Chapter 5

Difficult Times

As my children grew older, so did my parents, and they needed more and more help. In the mid-1990s, my stepfather was placed in a nursing home. He had Parkinson's, and staying home was not an option anymore. His care had advanced and become very difficult for Mom. His condition was not pleasant to watch; he seemed to waste away, trapped in a body that couldn't function, and communication was difficult. Mom was by his side almost every day. The staff had become her new family, and she loved the attention they gave her. She had adopted the staff and attended a wedding of a couple that worked there. My stepfather stayed at the nursing home for almost nine years.

One day the phone rang. My kids answered, but no one was there, so they hung up. After a few of these mysterious calls, I received a letter from my dad's new wife with information that led me to believe the calls were him. Apparently, he had a few heart attacks and a stroke that left him unable to speak. He wanted to make amends with me because he felt bad for walking out on me. This time it was him that felt rejection, in his time of amends, but it was too late for apologies in my opinion. He had lost contact with his other three children, and I was the only one he knew how to contact.

I wrote my dad's new wife a letter and explained as nicely as I could that I wanted nothing to do with him. That kind of pain he put me through was irreversible. I explained to her that my family was the most precious thing to me and I had moved on. I thought it was best for all of us. She wrote me back telling me that she understood. She had been in a similar situation.

Meanwhile, my stepfather's health declined. In 2001, we got a call in the middle of the night, and my husband and I got to the nursing home in time to be by his side the night he died. I called his oldest daughter to tell them he was gone.

Six weeks later, the phone rang, and I was told my adopted dad had died. His wife wanted me to know he was gone and that none of his other children could be contacted because they couldn't find them. I thanked her and gave my condolences but explained I wouldn't be able to attend his funeral. I had just experienced the loss of my stepfather.

This was a time when I reflected on the fact that as we were all aging, so was my birth mother, and I feared time was running out on us ever meeting.

A Place for Mom

In the years that followed, I remarried, my children grew up, and my mom's health worsened. In 2013 during a surgery to remove her gallbladder, my mom suffered a heart attack and came home on oxygen. In 2015, she fell while shopping and was taken to the hospital to have surgery on a broken left elbow; she had also broken her right kneecap. She was in the hospital for quite some time before coming to live with us for a month. During her recovery, she had a kidney stone and had a stent inserted. Once she was able to move back to her apartment, I checked on her weekly and took her shopping for supplies and medicines. At that time she was able to get around fairly well.

Throughout 2016, I visited her twice a week and set her up with Doorbell Dinners through the local hospital. Prior to that, she had been living on chocolate and cookies. But by 2017, I noticed a major decline in her mental status and knew we had to make a change. We had already taken over most of her affairs due to the lack of concern on her part. Bills weren't getting paid on time, her memory was fading, she wasn't eating properly, and she was forgetting basic needs. The worst problem was the scammers that continued to call her. She had no idea what was happening, and people were taking advantage of her. Her bank account had to be changed twice, and the bank threatened to close the account if it happened a third time. Her credit card had to be destroyed. I had to set up automatic bill payments and help with her mail so important stuff wasn't thrown away. Every time someone called, she was a target for cash or sales of any kind, and they knew it. The worst calls were magazine subscriptions sold by third parties. She said yes each time they called, and it was getting expensive. It wasn't easy to deal with. I couldn't disconnect her phone. I needed to reach her, and she needed to reach me. At first, I drove in three times each week, which left me totally worn out and unable to accomplish my own chores at home. My husband and I decided to build a small guest room for her at our house so she could remain as independent as possible.

In September 2018, my mom moved into her new living area. It was so cute, an open floor plan that my husband and I designed. She had lots of room to move around (but not too much). It was a fresh start. My whole life now revolved around the person who raised me. The one person I couldn't connect with. Our intentions were good, but this was going to be hard, we knew that from the start. If only she could accept me as an adult, her friend, it would be so much easier. She seemed jealous of who I had become and treated me as if I knew nothing. Always on the defense.

After the first two weeks, things went smoothly until the day she fell when company arrived. We had just gotten into a routine, and now she was at the hospital. She had broken her right wrist and surgery was not done. She had fallen several times. This was the second break, and no one seemed concerned about investigating why she was falling. The hospital sent her home, and that night she developed aspiration pneumonia. Back to the hospital we went, against her will. She didn't know how sick she was. This time my mom was admitted to the hospital but was discharged too soon. We would return to the hospital within twelve hours with congestive heart failure.

The surgery she needed on her wrist was never done. She was in significant pain each time she moved; her wrist was in a plaster cradle and healed on its own, leaving it very crooked. It was finally put in a plaster cast weeks after the fall and became extremely swollen. It was more than four times the size of her normal wrist, and no one offered to make her more comfortable. The cast was so tight it was causing an open sore on her hand. When the cast finally came off, I took my mom to the physical therapy department and asked for their opinion. Physical therapists worked with her several days a week to minimize her discomfort through the end of the year. We changed doctors to a more compassionate gentleman with a good bedside manner, a professional who was concerned about her well-being regardless of her age. It seems she was brushed off due to her age; I've seen it happen more than once in our health-care system over the years.

It was during this time that Mom's younger sister, Aunt Susie, asked me, "Have you ever thought about finding your real mother?" It didn't take long for this conversation to get under way. I felt so relieved that someone would ask about my birth mother. I had been coming to terms with the fact that I would never find my birth mother while caring for an aging parent—I had reached that point of no return.

I told Aunt Susie that in fact, I had been looking for my birth mother for many years but had kept running into brick walls. I was convinced it wasn't meant to be. She encouraged me to keep trying. Aunt Susie was an easy person to talk with, but she lived away from us, so our interactions were minimal. I often wish I had reached out to her more often for advice. She is fifteen years younger than my mom and didn't know my mom very well herself until their later years, when they would take mini-vacations off and on over the years. By then, they were well into their sixties and seventies. It was this very conversation with Aunt Susie that inspired me once again in wanting to find my birth mother. This time I had to think outside the box.

Chapter 6

Ancestry

I had already tried finding out more about my birth family on Ancestry back in the early 2000s. I hadn't joined full access because at that time Ancestry was still building its inventory and I was unable to find any useful information. But I was curious when I kept seeing an ad on the internet for 23andMe's DNA testing kit in late 2018. I ordered the kit and I waited and waited, but it never arrived in the mail. I was getting impatient, so I ordered the Ancestry DNA kit (at half cost!) during the holidays. It was delivered quickly, and I returned the sample with great anticipation. Soon I received confirmation that they had received my test and would have to wait six to eight long weeks for testing to be completed. I was skeptical but hopeful that this mystery of my birth family could be solved, knowing that after sixty-two years, this could very well be my last chance.

By January 2019, as I was waiting on the Ancestry results, Mom was getting back in the routine we had struggled to achieve prior to her fall. Things had finally settled down, but we still had obstacles to overcome. Mom's condition prevented her from knowing the dangers she was up against. The whole idea was to help her be as independent as possible but close by if there was a problem. She called us to assist her on several occasions. At times, she forgot how to use the phone and the TV. We checked on her multiple times throughout the day to make sure she got up each day, she got her medicines, food, and snacks, and her environment was clean and safe. To this day in 2022, she continues to be very defensive and unable to understand why we remind her of the daily needs we all take for granted. Her mind gets confused, and she struggles to comprehend what we are talking about. Some days are worse than others.

On February 2, 2019, I got the email that my Ancestry results were ready. I hesitated, nervous and excited at the same time, and then logged into my account. There it was: a person with a remarkable match, the closest DNA match of anyone in the Ancestry registry. I sent them a message and waited for a response.

A few days went by without a return message. I reached out to a few more people that appeared to be cousins with the next closest DNA match. Chances were that most people I paired with already knew their DNA matches. I was searching for a needle in a haystack. I knew I had to be careful with these messages; this was a sensitive subject, and I felt someone might see me as a threat or not respond at all.

You Have Mail

Then it happened! A message in my Ancestry email, followed by a few more. I kept the questions simple, and I only reached out to a few of the matches. One really sweet lady named Anita appeared to be my second cousin on my father's side. She was a tremendous help. Anita knew a lot of the people I was looking for because we shared great-grandparents. I was intrigued—my first conversation with a relative! She sent me a picture of the family gathering from 1920 and a copy of the family tree. This was my first photo, and I was delighted to be looking into faces from my family's past. Our great-grandparents were seated in the middle of the photo surrounded by many relatives, and my biological father's mother was there. It was outstanding to see my grandmother as a child.

The two of us messaged each other quite often and even shared several phone conversations. I liked Anita a lot. She was in charge of her family tree and the reunions. She made sure all family members were carefully entered in her family records, and she was full of information. Together we plotted and schemed like Nancy Drew trying to solve a mystery. My husband smiled each time she called.

I reached out to a random, non-related person that seemed to know her way around Ancestry. She had made a huge family tree of her own. She emailed me back and included all my family members' names, towns, birthdays, a phone number and, best of all, my birth mother's married name. She gave me directions on how to reach my family and how to contact my mother. Also, my sister, Sheryl, was on Facebook!

I tried calling the phone number that was supposed to be my birth mother's most recent number. No one answered. I left a few messages but received no call back. On Saturday, February 16, 2019, I sent Sheryl a friend request on Facebook before I went to bed. By the time I woke up on Sunday morning, she had friended me.

I sent her a private message with details and hoped she'd answer me soon. I waited for her to read the message. The message read:

"Hello, my name is Leeanne Swain from Illinois. I have a story for you, and you may want to sit down. I wasn't always Leeanne. On August 8, 1956, I was born D. J., and my birth mother was —— Horton, who had a sister. I would very much like to meet this lady. My son was born thirty-eight years ago with a heart defect, and my adoption records were opened. A very nice lady from Ancestry.com has helped me locate you. If you need time to process this, I totally understand. I am on Facebook, and my phone number is ———. I find it hard to believe that this person wouldn't want to meet me again after all these years. She held me after I was born, and the night I was born there was a terrible storm and the power went out and the hospital generator came on. The night I was born, the sister sat down with Sarah, the lady they were renting from (who I have spoken to over twenty-five years ago), and mentioned some details. Her mother was a twin, she had three brothers, and they were headed back to the East Coast."

On February 23, Sheryl read my message. I waited patiently, hoping for a response. My biggest fear was that I would scare her off.

The truth is: when I found my sister, I found myself, and things started to fall in place. With each photo I saw of Sheryl, I saw myself at a younger age. It was like looking in a mirror. My children saw the resemblance too; they were surprised, and there was no doubt in our minds we were family.

With full access to Ancestry, I found my birth mother's high school yearbook picture. I told my husband as I showed him the picture, "Trust me, this is my mama." We looked very much alike except for the color of our hair. Hers was dark brown and mine was dishwater blonde, but the shape of our faces, right down to our crooked teeth, were identical. There was no mistaking the resemblance.

Moment of Contact

My phone rang on Monday, February 25 around five thirty in the evening. I was in the kitchen doorway, headed to Mom's with her supper. My husband was eating at the table. I looked at my phone and stopped in my tracks. It was a call from New York. My mouth dropped open; I hesitated before answering. My husband looked up from the table, worried, and asked if I was all right. Unable to speak, my heart pounding in my chest, I answered the phone. It was then my husband knew everything was good—my sister was calling.

We talked, we cried, we laughed; she was unaware all these years that she had an older sister. Sheryl said she had always wanted a sister. She told me we had a younger brother also. I scolded her for friending someone she didn't know (me), and her response was, "I know, but your picture on Facebook was so cute of the two of you." She told me she often felt like something was missing when she was growing up. After processing the message I had sent her, she says her life started to fall in place. Things just didn't add up on her end about why her (our) mama had waited so long to start a family.

It was Sheryl's son, my nephew, that I was a close match with on Ancestry. He was hoping to expand his family. I was grateful for his curiosity. Otherwise, we might not have met so quickly. Sheryl apologized for not calling sooner, but she had needed to talk to a few family members. I told her how much I needed her in my life. I already loved her and how much she looked like me when I was her age. She could tell from my message that every little detail matched with her family, and her first cousin had the same name I had been given at birth.

She hadn't mentioned our mama. Taking a deep breath, I asked her, "Is my mommy okay?"

With somewhat of a chuckle and the sound of tears in her voice, Sheryl replied, "Yeah, she's playing bingo."

"What? Bingo? That's great!" I said.

She was alive and well. Meaning I might get to meet my mama after all. I asked if our mama knew I had found her. Sheryl told me Mama H had access to her Facebook page, so probably she had seen the message. I hadn't planned on giving anyone a heart attack, but this was a big deal. Our conversation went on for over an hour. Neither of us wanted to hang up that first phone call.

At that point, the past wasn't so important; we hoped to get acquainted. I was on cloud nine. We had bonded, and I felt like a new person. I hoped Sheryl wouldn't pressure our mama into answering too many questions too soon. I feared she might make Mama H angry or resentful and push her away from me. Sheryl and I talked off and on over the next few weeks and messaged each other. We sent many pictures back and forth, introducing family members and sharing baby pictures to compare resemblances.

I wasn't able to talk with my mama the times I called her house. I trusted Sheryl to communicate with her and hoped she would accept me. While I waited, I could only imagine how hard it would be for my mama to reveal the story of me to our family. I wanted so badly to speak with her and see her. I had met her once on the day of my birth, but only she had that memory of our brief encounter. I had grown up a lot since that day. I was so sure my mama was curious and would rather meet me in person.

Chapter 7

When Dreams Come True

One day in early March 2019, my sister, Sheryl, called and asked if we would be home because she was coming to see me. I asked if she would bring Mama H along for company, but she wasn't sure. Maybe she'd change her mind? Maybe they would surprise me? The day before my sister left New York, I just couldn't wait; I had to know if Mama H would come with her. Later that night I got her response: our mama said yes! I was going to be face to face with my mama within hours. I was now sixty-two years old and ready to meet my mama all over again. The adult version of me was all I had to offer, with only pictures to fill in the blanks. Over forty years of searching had come to an end.

As I waited at my house for my sister and Mama H to show up, the wind blew and blew. It seemed fitting considering the last time my mama and I were together was the dark and stormy night of my birth. I was on the phone with my daughter waiting for their arrival; I had expected them a few hours before. She was eager to know if they had arrived before she went to work. I walked to the back porch to look down the road, and for a moment my heart stopped. I saw a car had stopped alongside our road. I told my daughter it was a car I didn't recognize—wait, it's moving, going slow, and then it pulled into our driveway. I hung up. It was them; they had out-of-state license plates. It had to be them. They were here!

Mama H arrives for our first visit after sixty-two years

Sheryl's artwork *A Million Dreams Are Coming True*

My husband headed outside to greet them in the wind. I was frozen in my tracks on the porch, wanting to move but watching from a distance for a minute. I slowly moved to open the door. My sister ran up to me and hugged me close in a giant bear hug. We were so happy! My mama was trying to get a look at the woman I'd become, and I motioned her to join the hug. The wind was deafening. That stormy, windy night over sixty years before seemed like an eternity ago, but it was happening all over again. We were face to face, all three of us, with the wind blowing us sideways. My husband took pictures of our reunion. Both Sheryl and Mama H had to get a look at my eyes, my blue eyes. I had my grandmother's blue eyes, we all did, and they were very excited to see that. We headed into the house to escape the unpleasant wind.

So Much in Common

Right away, I noticed traits we shared, all of us. We all wore glasses but not to read; we had wraparound sunglasses, and Mama H had a pair just like mine. She loved Honey Nut Cheerios and room-temperature water just like me. We both enjoyed hot dogs, Rice Krispies bars, ginger ale, and marshmallows roasted over an open fire. Our baby fine hair was the same texture and almost the same color. We liked to collect bunnies and snowmen, and she had a collection of trolls and dolls. She had collected more trolls than I had. We enjoyed the outdoors, fishing, and wildlife, and we were both quiet, private people. Mama H was an average bowler, but me, not so much. I was presented with a trophy for the most gutter balls in my thirties. They could drive a stick shift, unlike me. Mama H was a real bingo player; I had only played as a child. She lived on tomato sandwiches while pregnant with me and—actually, I don't like tomatoes; we all laughed. My sister loves lighthouses and squealed as she entered our bathroom, as it is decorated with lighthouses all over the walls and a large wooden lighthouse sits inside the doorway.

Mama H liked coffee, but not too strong or hot, and dark rooms without bright lights. We all had to carry water at all times even by our bedside. These similarities kept repeating themselves; it was so clear to me that I was with my people and I had found my family.

We researched our ancestors online, huddled together over the computer. At the same time, the three of us removed our glasses to read articles. My husband chuckled as he watched. It was as if we had known each other forever—our mannerisms were alike.

During their stay, Mama H said things to me that were sincere, things I needed to hear so badly. She accepted all of us, she loved us, she said I was kind, a gift from God. It was a surprise to me when she told me it wasn't her that picked out the name that appears on my documents. We thought that her sister might have given the nurse that name because her sister named her firstborn child that same name. Mama H had wanted to name me Brenda Lee, but the nurse never came back to ask her again. I learned from

my mama I had not been forgotten. She thought of me often, especially when she traveled through Illinois to visit family out west.
There was a time when she imagined I would find her. The years
passed, and so did her idea of meeting me. Her thought was that I
had no interest in finding her, when in fact I was struggling to do
just that, find her. I believe it was a huge relief for her to unburden
after all these years. She hadn't told anyone because there would
never be a good time, and as the years went by, it became irrele-
vant. I know she was just as curious about me as I was of her, and
the truth is, fate somehow brought us together.

I watched how my sister and our mama carried on a normal
conversation, trying to remember details of past memories. They
were both calm, no drama, no harsh tones in their voices, and they
spoke in harmony. They acted like best friends, needing each other's company and valuing each other's opinion. They shared ideas
and memories calmly. Just the kind of relationship I longed for
between a mother and daughter.

Mama H was patient with me and listened without judging or
blaming me. She was quiet and calm. For the first time in my life, I
was able to call her Mommy, hug her, and kiss her. It was a special
day, a day I would have missed had I given up my search. I told her
how hard it was to get information and how the doctor's office was
not nice about it. She was not at all upset that I had tried to collect
her information. She was more upset they had given me a hard
time in doing so. Genetics is hard to break. I found myself to be
more like my mama, in spite of the fact that the two of us had never
spent any time together before the visit.

Mama H handed me a picture of herself at two years old. I was
speechless. If only I'd had that picture while I was growing up, I
could have reflected on my past with a tangible connection. That
picture meant the world to me. It was as if we were twins separated
at birth. My heart was filled with great joy. We shared some family
medical history. I told her I was sick the first eight years of my life
and had recently found out I have a faulty immune system.

She praised me for taking care of my mom, giving me approval and making me feel good about myself. With a wink of her eye and a nod of her head, Mama H told me what I was doing was a good thing, just like a proud mother would. She told me about the time she cared for her own grandmother when she was sick with a severe case of shingles.

Sheryl went public on Facebook about finding a long-lost sister, and the response was overwhelming. What my mama had feared all these years didn't happen—no one was angry. It was time to put the past behind her because now everyone wanted to meet me. I do believe Mama H was greatly relieved that after all these years her children were together at last and that everyone knew about me. I'm sure she thought her family would be angry and even shame her. Instead, they were happy, understanding, and welcoming.

All days must end, and this one ended with a windy surprise. Just after dark, the wind blew fiercely and the lights flickered; for an instant, we were in total darkness. The sound of a tree crashing down literally shook the foundation of our house. We went outside with a flashlight to find a big tree and a smaller one both resting just a few feet from my sister's car. After moving her car, we found everything else to be in order. We waited for the wind to calm down over the next few hours and laughed as we told Mama H this was because she was back in Illinois. It was for sure a coincidence.

Meeting Illinois Family

My daughter was the first of my children to meet her Aunt Sheryl and her grandmother. It was a short visit but a magical one. She was speechless. The look on her face was priceless as she saw the resemblance that my sister and I had when I was her age. She approached them standing in our living room and said, "Oh my gosh, you look like my mom when I was growing up, wow!"

Sheryl turned to our mama and introduced her: "Mom, this is your granddaughter." My heart was happy as I watched them smile and hug.

All my children and grandchildren were able to come to my house that Saturday to meet my mama and sister. The family grew in size that day as we posed for our very first family photo. Mama H wore a huge smile as she stood surrounded by all her newest family members. In her own words, she was elated! Her family grew larger that day with me, my husband, three new grandchildren, five great-grandsons, and one bonus great-grandchild. It was incredible! My mama met my mom and thanked her for raising such a good, kind person. Mom said, "Thank you, I wasn't able to have my own." Mama H told Mom that she had a nice little place, and Mom gave her a tour, grateful for the company.

My mom and Mama H hugging while thanking each other during our very first visit in 2019

When it came time for everyone to part ways, both my mama and my mom hugged one another and smiled to each other. I was able to get a picture of that hug. They were almost identical in size and height and were both in their eighties. Even in their younger days, my mom and mama appeared somewhat similar with the same hair color and smiles on their faces. I remember Mom telling me years ago that the doctor said she was a good match for me. I couldn't believe my eyes; even now I could see how correct he was. That hug was emotional for Sheryl and me; we cried a few times that weekend. As my children and grandchildren left one by one, I heard one grandson shout out to me, "Hey Grandma, I like your sister, and your mother's really nice too."

First family photo at our house with
all my family members in Illinois

Of course, no visit is complete without a trip to the local Walmart. It was a special treat when the checkout lady made the comment, "You must be daughter, mother, and grandmother."

We were all smiles. Sheryl gave me a big hug and said, "We're sisters."

And I said, "This is our mom." We are family together—how precious is that! A total stranger saw the resemblance between the three of us.

A Newsworthy Story

Our first meeting in March 2019 was a happy one. I was so excited to share the news of my search for my birth mother that I contacted a local newspaper, and they wrote a story on us. It made the front page. The reporter did an excellent job writing the article and even included a photo taken during our visit.

After this article was published, Anita sent a copy of it to my dad's youngest sister and introduced me as her niece. Contact from my dad's side was about to take place. I hadn't planned on that, but my attitude was "Why not?" We are all adults. There are close-minded people that make it hard to talk about sensitive subjects, like those I ran into during my journey. They only see things in black and white and aren't open to other possibilities. I assumed I could reach out to my dad's side of my family for some health history and leave it at that. In the meantime, there were other family members to meet back in New York, and I was eager to meet them all.

Time passed so quickly during that first visit. I wasn't ready for Mama H and Sheryl to leave when the time came. We had already started planning our visit to New York before they even left the house.

Chapter 8

New York Visit

In June 2019, my husband and I, along with our family cat, traveled to the hills of Upstate New York to meet my birth family. The drive was long. Along the way, we talked about our trip to Niagara Falls and New York City back in 2001 just after 9/11, during the final two weeks of cleanup. I realized that all those years ago, we had practically driven through my family's backyards as we drove down from New York to Pennsylvania. To think my family had been here all along!

Before we knew it, we were crossing a mountain, and I was overwhelmed by the beauty in front of us. The small town of Watkins Glen was full of charm and short, winding roads that are tiny and hilly. It was the beginning of tourist season, and the roads were bustling. Vineyards and wineries dotted the hills, and we passed Amish stands with wares to sell and beekeepers with honey for sale at different houses. I could feel the charm of country living in the Finger Lakes region.

This was the place I might have grown up if things had been different. It felt like such a good fit. Everything I could have hoped for was here. The air was clean; the hills were all around us. A true miracle was happening, nothing but joy and celebration with peace and harmony. This area was full of beauty. As we drove toward my sister's house, I kept thinking, I could have been so happy here. I

LA Swain

loved everything about this place—the mountains, the climate, the quaint little villages.

Welcome to the Family

We arrived on June 22, a Saturday, and camped out in my sister's front yard. Sheryl told me I was like a celebrity and people were curious to meet me. I didn't feel special at all. I just wanted to meet my family, get to know them, and hang out for a few days.

We did so many things during our visit, and Sheryl and her family did make us feel special. Her bubbling energy was that of a bottle of champagne. Her creativity inspired me, and her ability to draw interesting designs was enchanting. She made a delicious baked spaghetti, which was new to us, and the aroma filled the house. Sheryl introduced me to Chocolate Lab wine, which is much better than it sounds—it has a hint of a chocolate flavor. It was obvious she was making every effort to make us feel at home, and she succeeded with flying colors.

I met my brother and his beautiful daughter, my niece. I couldn't believe that even he looked like me! Our faces have the same characteristics of our mama's and sister's faces. There was no doubt we were related, and I was smitten with joy. Taking pictures with my siblings and our mama was so special. I often look back through the pictures to see how much we look alike—our faces, our hair color, and even our mannerisms. The only difference I can see is that we all grew taller than her. What I also see in this first family photo of my New York family is my brother being silly as he gave me bunny ears like brothers do.

Someone commented that if we had grown up as siblings, we might have hated each other. I would hope that wouldn't have been the case. I was an only child with a wish of having a brother or sister. Growing up, I had no idea of what having a sibling was like. But standing next to my brother and sister, I can't say I felt like a half person to either one of my siblings; I felt like we were one hundred percent related. After all, we all three came from the same factory, Mama H; they were brand name, and I was generic. I continue to

Mama H with her three children on Sheryl's front porch

be amused by the facial expressions and actions that are so much alike. Even our likes and dislikes, it's just who we are.

As I watched this family—my family—interacting, I cherished this glimpse of what I'd missed as a child. Finally, I wasn't trying to blend in; this was my family, I was accepted. My heart melted as I watched the smiles and heard the laughter and conversation that flowed so effortlessly. Everyone was happy.

Our first cousin brought with her a black-and-white picture of my grandmother and her twin. It was taken when they were close to eighteen months old (I can only guess, as there are no details pertaining to this photo except for my great-grandmother's name on the back of the photo board). When I compared the baby pictures to mine, I saw my grandma's face in me. I had known my grandmother was a twin for many years and had hoped I might have a set of twins. Mama H agreed and felt the same way; she would have liked a set of twins also.

Mama H told me she couldn't get over how much alike Sheryl and I were. It amazed both of us that it was so noticeable. During a moment alone, Mama H quietly asked me if my life was good because I seemed fine. "Fine"—a word I had become so familiar with, one I used quite often to describe how I felt because it seemed like the perfect word for not exploring how I really felt. I told her I didn't want to hurt her feelings, but I was honest and told her that my dad walked out on me when I was two. I didn't have a dad till I was eight, a stepfather. I told her how much I really needed

My grandma Horton (left) with her twin when they were toddlers

her but that in spite of her absence, she made me strong. It was my goal to make her proud at all times, and she helped me become the person I am. She was always a part of my life, even in her absence. I had refused to let the world change the person I was inside. My life had taken a sudden detour when I was a baby, but now I felt like it was on track.

No matter what I said, Mama H encouraged me to get it out and to feel better. She comforted me calmly and said, "Let it out, you need to." It meant so much to me that she cared about me and listened to me and was able to validate my feelings.

That evening, we enjoyed a huge fire out back. While we sat around the fire, hypnotized by the tall orange flames, thoughts crossed my mind. I really enjoyed the serenity of the area and imagined myself being content growing up there in New York. The evening got cooler, but I welcomed the cool temperatures. I felt so content sitting around the fire with my family, watching the dogs run around the yard. It seemed that each family member had dogs and brought them to our celebration. I joked, "Wow, everyone and their dogs really did come to our party!"

Exploring Our Family History

That next morning, we woke up to the smell of an apple pie my sister had made. It was beautiful and delicious. We visited my grandma and grandpa's house, which was built in 1875 in Pine Valley, where my cousin now lives. I was thankful it was still in the family and I could walk inside and see Mama H's bedroom and where she had grown up. In the meadow was a shell of an old truck, and trees had grown right through the middle of the frame. My grandfather was hit by a train while driving that truck, and he survived without any injuries.

Next stop, Mama H's house where my sister and brother grew up. Mama H told us the story that was told to her by her family of our ancestors who sailed the seas on a family ship from England, making several trips back and forth to this New World before it came to rest at the bottom of the sea like so many others.

We had uncovered some of this family history together during her visit to Illinois earlier in the year. During their visit, my mama, sister, and I had spent time on Ancestry looking for facts about our past generations. Our research uncovered some incredible details. We traced my mama's side of the family back to the 1600s. The first Horton to come to America, Barnabas Horton, sailed here from England around 1635–38 on a family ship, the *Swallow*, captained by his brother. It appears we are descendants of this mysterious man, connected over the years by seven men from century to century. After reaching the New World, Barnabas Horton crossed the Sound and settled on the northeast shore of what came to be known as Long Island in 1640. He and several other families were the first people to claim ground on what would later be named New York. His original homestead is said to be one of the first and oldest framed houses built alongside the North Bay of the Southold hamlet around 1640. This house was demolished, but one wall was saved and relocated to be restored into a house somewhere close by.

In 1790, George Washington commissioned a lighthouse to be built on the land granted to Barnabas. Although it wasn't built until many years later in 1857, it was named Horton Point Lighthouse. It is now a nautical museum maintained by the Southold Historical Society. Many whaling ships were lost at sea from the debris and boulders off the sandy shores that lay below a sixty-foot cliff of this place called Dead Man's Cove. By the lighthouse is the old cemetery, North Burial Ground. Some of our family's earliest settlers of this land remain there to this day, reminding us of our past that started with Barnabas Horton, 1600–1680. He was a great leader, perhaps a person of great wealth in early days, who was a baker by trade and performed many important duties in his community.

Over the years, our ancestors continued to travel into Upstate New York. Small towns mark the trail along the way—some are named after our family, such as Horton, New York. One of the original houses is no longer in the family as it was lost during the gold rush days on a bad bet; it was owned at the time by Uncle John. This town also has a cemetery named after the family, Horton Cemetery.

Mama H showed us a very old portrait from 1893 of the Horton homestead; it is labeled quite clearly, but we aren't sure of its location. In the photo is my third great-grandma Huldah. She was Native American, Iroquois (Seneca) of New York. Also called the Great Hill People, this large group lived in longhouses along the riverbanks. The portrait shows two men close by Huldah with a longhouse in the background.

More family migrated further up into the state close to the Seneca Lake area, including my great-grandmother who came to this country on a boat from Germany. Mama H had taken care of her when she had a severe case of shingles. We learned about ancestors that blazed a trail many years before us. It meant so much to me to learn about those family members from my ancestry and take a journey into my past. Now, I have a few of those pictures in my family album and I can look into the faces of our past, knowing they are family from long ago.

The Beauty of Upstate New York

Later that day, we hiked through Watkins Glen State Park to see the gorge and its amazing waterfalls and gorgeous scenery. The gorge was carved by a glacier back in the Ice Age of the Pleistocene epoch. It plunges four hundred feet into a narrow gorge cut from the water of Glen Creek. This state park covers 778 acres and was first opened in 1863. It was a breathtaking experience as we walked along a trail deeper into the earth and heard the power of the water rushing down the cliffs and swirling through the rocks. The sounds are deafening but at the same time relaxing.

Photo of me entering the gorge in
2019 during our New York visit

There are many huge waterfalls all around the park; some are visible from the main roads, while others are tucked away, hidden from the public, and only the locals know where to find them. Hector Falls cascades down a 165-foot cliff flowing under Route 414. This is a busy highway, and you can hear the roar of the waterfall as you're driving by. Another huge waterfall is in the town of Montour, a small mountain town with tiny streets that are almost unable to handle the number of tourists it attracts. Most of these small towns are all alike in their small-town presence, being quaint and inviting.

We took a boat ride on Seneca Lake with our mama. Lake Seneca is the deepest and largest Finger Lake (618 feet deep) of the eleven in the region. Formed by the glaciers more than two million years ago, it's a huge body of water that connects to the Erie Canal and finds its way to the Atlantic Ocean. They say you can travel the world from here due to the canal passages. The lake water flows northward, eventually making its way to Lake Ontario.

Our group onboard the *Stroller IV*

On the boat ride, we passed by the salt plant off the shore where Mama H worked for many years. The boat is named the *Stroller IV*, christened in 1934 and owned by Captain Bill. It's a vintage forty-nine passenger mahogany vessel and offers tours that are about an hour long during the sightseeing season. On the tour, a narrator showed us the sights and told us the history of the lake and area. He pointed out the Native American rock paintings on the eastern cliffs that can only be seen from the water.

Playing Bingo with Mama H

During our visit in New York, we played professional bingo at a real bingo hall in Horseheads with our mama. It was so busy and filled with people. I had no idea bingo could go on for three hours and that it was so complicated.

The bingo hall was where I met Aunt B, my mama's sister. During the bingo break, Sheryl and I walked over to the table where Aunt B and two of her daughters, my cousins, sat. Aunt B's oldest daughter asked her if she knew who I was.

"Well, she's got to be family—she looks just like my sister," Aunt B said.

I greeted her and said, "Maybe that's because I'm that baby you two left in Jacksonville, Illinois, sixty-two years ago."

Keep in mind, that was a topic no one had talked about over the years. She threw her arms around me. As she hugged me close and gave me kisses, Aunt B told me she loved me and would have kept me. She told me what a beautiful baby I was. I had never heard anything like it before; it was monumental for me. My sister invited them over to eat the next night.

After bingo, Mama H wanted Sheryl to take me to the cemetery where her parents (my grandparents) are buried. Afterward, we drove by the grade school and then the high school that my brother and sister attended. We had our first adventure with just the two of us. We entered the back entrance to the high school by the bus barn and noticed the gates were shut. (Since 9/11, a lot of places are on lockdown, and the schools were no different.) Beside the gate, two cop cars were sitting side by side. As Sheryl did a U-turn, I waved at the cops and smiled into their headlights, and you guessed it, the red lights came on and we were pulled over. They let us go after Sheryl explained she was showing her school to her sister who was visiting from out of state. We laughed all the way to her house, eager to share our encounter with the men.

Later in the trip, we made it to one of the many beaches along Lake Seneca and searched for beach glass, flat rocks, and driftwood. The beach glass had been on my list of things to do. All around us were flat gray rocks unlike any in our area. The water was cold for June, but it was still relaxing to walk the waterline.

We also visited some older cemeteries on top of big hills. One had the gravesite of my sister's oldest son who was five years old when he died. Twenty-two years ago, a careless driver hit them head on. My sister was injured badly and unable to work for a very long time. Her son once told her, "I want to be a kid forever." His birthday is in August, just two days after mine.

Our visit to New York was over in the blink of an eye. There wasn't enough time, but we managed to do quite a lot while we were there. Most of all I felt love, the key ingredient. I had this once-in-a-lifetime opportunity, and it was time for acceptance and family. That experience opened a window into my soul.

Perhaps this is when I became real; I had just met my mom weeks before and we had just visited the place I might have called home, had things been different and I hadn't been given away. In all life's turmoil, I had lost my shine and I suddenly found it again.

Chapter 9

Family Visits

On September 9, 2019, I met my biological father for the first time. He had died just a few years before my search was complete, so I missed the opportunity to meet him face to face. I met my biological father through a picture of him by an old truck with a guitar on his knee. He appeared to be wearing army fatigues from his military service. He had a kind face and was somewhat handsome. I was told he played gospel songs on his guitar; his mother didn't allow any other music in their house. I am sure he played some country songs as he grew older. He was from a large family of nine children, six boys and three girls. He was the oldest.

My father's youngest sister was going to be in our area for a few days, and she wanted to meet me. We met briefly on August 22, 2019, but they were skeptical that my story was true. I don't blame them since my father is no longer here to confirm the story, yet here I am. After this meeting, she sent me some photos of my father and a few other members of the family. It was nice to have these photos. Most of the children's baby pictures were lost in a house fire when she was younger.

She also reached out to my father's children and encouraged them to contact me. They had a positive attitude and wanted to meet me. We met during our 2019 Thanksgiving trip to New York. It was a good visit; they seemed to have many talents and were in good health. A positive DNA match would later confirm for them that my story was true.

My only intention was to find my mama, but there seemed to be more DNA matches from my father's side. With all these new connections with both my birth mother's and father's sides, I was able to complete my family health history. All my life I hadn't been able to complete a family health history and had to explain at doctor's offices why I didn't have one. I am grateful for these contacts and to everyone that welcomed my children and grandchildren into their lives. I am now on my father's family tree with all its family members.

More Visits in Illinois and New York

Mama H and Sheryl returned to our house in late September 2019 for a short visit. We visited the nearby small town of New Salem, where President Abraham Lincoln stayed from 1831 to 1837. The streets are lined with log cabin homes like an old-time village. It was a trip back in time, and my mama enjoyed herself. Later that day we ate at Capone's Hideout, a family owned and operated restaurant in New Berlin, Illinois, not far from our house.

We traveled back to New York around Thanksgiving in 2019 because I had heard that Uncle Walt, Mama H's brother, was coming to visit the week prior. We had a wonderful meal, an early holiday dinner. Smells of good food and all the trimmings filled the house as my sister cooked a big turkey and Mama H made a pecan pie from the pecans my uncle brings each year from South Carolina. We even had some homemade corn tamales. Sheryl read a Native American prayer before the meal, and it brought me to tears. It was the best holiday I had ever shared with anyone before and a very emotional moment.

Uncle Walt kept us entertained with a discussion on the pronunciation of nut names. He asked, "How do you say pecan?" Depending on where you live, some people pronounce it with a long *a*, while others use a short *a*. The proper way is his way, of course.

When we returned home from New York, I tried to tell my children about these amazing stories that Uncle Walt shared with us. They said it would be better if they heard them from him.

Uncle Walt Comes to Illinois

My children and grandchildren got their wish. They met their Uncle Walt at our house during the spring of 2021, a year into the COVID-19 pandemic that paralyzed the world. His stories came to life, as he had so many to share with them. We all listened in silence, hanging on to each word he spoke.

Uncle Walt was in the military and served in the Korean War with the army. He was very proud of his service from 1954 to 1956. After his discharge, he continued for six months with the reserve.

It sounded like he was quite a fisherman. He entertained us with a story of fishing with his brother. Uncle Walt speared a twenty-six-pound landlocked salmon in their backyard in the historic Catharine Creek that ran through the meadow behind the barn. The spear broke, and the fish floated off downstream. They looked for it but had no luck finding it. The next day on the front page of the local newspaper was a picture of that huge fish. Someone else had found it and claimed it. My uncle showed his father the paper and told him they recognized it by the broken spear sticking out of its side. They would fish for gars with long noses and short noses, each being edible. They have no bones in them, just a spine. We were instructed on how to clean them so the meat wasn't tough. He even mentioned they ate groundhogs—what a terrible thought.

Uncle Walt and his brother spent many days playing cowboys and Indians with cattail arrows and BB guns. His older brother dared him to shoot one of the family chickens from an unreasonable distance and, you guessed it, he did. He used a .22 from a half mile away. He ran to the house to tell his mother not to tell his father of what just transpired or he would have his hide. She told Walt she would tell his father it was her idea to have chicken for dinner that night. The story goes that at times Walt and his brother might have even shot at each other, but we won't go into that. They were boys from the old days.

He had a friend who knew a mafia family member. I was so fascinated I could barely keep up. At one time, Uncle Walt played the Madagascar Man in a carnival one summer in New York. He also played a small part in the movie *The Phenix City Story* in 1955; he was guarding a bridge in Alabama during the time he was in the army.

He reminded everyone that my third great-grandmother was a full-blooded Native American. Uncle Walt had a Native American name of "Deer Slayer," given to him back in his younger days when he was surveying a major highway out west in Nevada. A Native American gave him that name when he ran after and killed a small deer. The story, as told to us, was that deer head hung high on the wall behind the counter of a local bar in Nevada.

He drove a 2017 red Mustang. He was proud of that car! He was a young man at heart and very loving, full of stories from his colorful past. His most epic story of all was racing against Dale Earnhardt in a stock car back in the late fifties at Watkins Glen track before Earnhardt became famous. My uncle won that race!

I could picture that race because during our visit in June 2019, we had driven by the Watkins Glen racetrack, located on a wooded hilltop southwest of town. It was isolated in the middle of nowhere. The original track in 1948, known as Watkins Glen Grand Prix, was a 6.6-mile course that went right through town. The roads were shut down during race day, and people lined the streets to watch and cheer the drivers on. We drove on a portion of the old track, and it seemed very dangerous with small, narrow turns and blind corners lined by rocky mountains; there was even a bridge to cross. Due to some casualties, the track was relocated to where it is today as a road course. It has grown in popularity over the years, and well-known race drivers return each year. Its name was changed to Watkins Glen International as it supports many types of racing today.

I lost my Uncle Walt during the pandemic (March 19, 1936–February 14, 2022). He will be missed very much by all of us, but I'm glad my children and grandchildren met him and heard his stories. He was delighted to have his stories in print. It made him so happy.

Uncle Walt in his red Mustang

Short but Sweet

That first year of 2019, I had four short but great visits together with my birth family. Then the COVID-19 pandemic hit during the spring of 2020 in the US and put a damper on any travel we might consider. Trying to find someone to watch Mom is a problem. We are doing our best to keep her safe.

I hope to have many more visits with my newfound family in the future, but the distance haunts me. The devastating COVID-19 pandemic did a number on everyone and it seemed to affect many aspects of our lives. We are now in recovery, but this may be a situation we must continue to watch very closely and it will become a new part of our world, a new normal.

Life is not a destination but rather a journey, and along the way I found my mama. My lifelong wish has been granted, and I continue to be amazed with all the details about my family history we have learned. I have visited my past, and it is filled with even more than I could have imagined. I feel blessed.

Epilogue

My story began at a small hospital in Jacksonville, Illinois, in 1956. Mama H had traveled with her sister from five states away and left me to be raised by another woman. A total stranger was about to teach me what she understood about the world from her point of view. It was up to me to figure it out. What I figured out was that I needed my birth mother more than anything else. I felt out of place in a huge world full of chaos.

I learned about my adoption at a young age. Many days I wished it weren't true. I wanted my real family surrounding me like my friends whose family members had similar interests and characteristics and most of all looked like each other. I wanted brothers and sisters so I would have a friend for life. I often wished I had never been told that I was adopted. I felt cheated and left behind. I felt like a possession rather than a person. I was denied a normal life with my family but remained hopeful that someday I might meet this person, my birth mother. I had to sort out a lot of difficult thoughts. I would later begin the most difficult challenge of my life, the search for my mama. To find her was a dream—until it became reality.

Adoption seems like a good solution, but I can speak from experience that it also comes with a price. It's always the child who suffers, no matter the situation. My situation left me full of anxiety and feeling alone. My anxiety will always need to be managed; there always seems to be a trigger, especially during stressful times. I do believe this journey has been a big help as I continue to mend my spirits.

I read an article a while back that explained we all need a past upon which to reflect. No matter at what age you are placed with an adoptive family, you bring a past with you. I was adopted at birth, unaware of my past. This is what leaves some people feeling lost. We need a bridge that connects the past to the present so we can move into the future feeling complete. That bridge is our story. It brings a sense of belonging so we can move forward.

I felt that sense of belonging when Mama H stood in front of me in our kitchen and said, "I'm glad you didn't stop looking for me!" I could tell she meant it by the huge smile on her face. That was exactly what I needed to hear! After meeting my mama and my family and connecting with my past and family history in New York, I can say that I finally feel at peace. All the information I spent years gathering led me to writing this book. Little did I know that writing a book would be a form of healing for my soul. My past and present are connected, and I can move forward into the future feeling like I belong.

One might say I became Real—something that takes years happened to me in an instant.

"Once you are Real, you can't become unreal again. It lasts for always."

—Margery Williams, *The Velveteen Rabbit*

Mama and I during one of her visits

Acknowledgments

Thank you to all the family and/or friends who may have helped in the making of this book, especially to the publisher and editor who helped it come to life.

About the Author

Leeanne Swain has self-published several children's books and a family cookbook. After spending a lifetime in the health-care field, she is married and lives on a Midwestern grain farm with her supportive husband. He is her ideal partner and soulmate, and they enjoy the company of several fur babies. Her children are grown with kids of their own and all live nearby.

Leeanne's hobbies include cooking, baking, knitting, crocheting, crafting, and photography, to name a few. She also enjoys caring for her loved ones.

www.ingramcontent.com/pod-product-compliance
Lightning Source LLC
Chambersburg PA
CBHW031249120626
46545CB00007B/2719